The BIG TEXAS REPRODUCIBLE Activity Book!

BY CAROLE MARSH

This activity book has material which correlates with (TEKS) Texas Essential Knowledge and Skills.

At every opportunity, we have tried to relate information to the History and Social Science, English, Science, Math, Civics, Economics, and Computer Technology TEKS directives.

For additional information, go to our websites: **www.texasexperience.com** or **www.gallopade.com**.

Published by
GALLOPADE™
INTERNATIONAL

800-536-2GET
www.gallopade.com

Connect to a world of related information, activities, and more at:
www.gallopade.com/techconnects.html
Password: activity

Gallopade is proud to be a member or supporter of these educational organizations and associations:

NSSEA   ASCD   ABA AMERICAN BOOKSELLERS ASSOCIATION   APPL SUPPORTER   NCSS

Cover character illustrations © Dawn Hudson | Agency: Dreamstime.com

A Word From The Author

Texas is a very special state. Almost everything about Texas is interesting and fun! It has a remarkable history that helped create the great nation of America. Texas enjoys an amazing geography of incredible beauty and fascination. The state's people are unique and have accomplished many great things.

This Activity Book is chockful of activities to entice you to learn more about Texas. While completing mazes, dot-to-dots, word searches, coloring activities, word codes, and other fun-to-do activities, you'll learn about Texas' history, geography, people, places, animals, legends, and more.

Whether you're sitting in a classroom, stuck inside on a rainy day, or—better yet—sitting in the back seat of a car touring the wonderful state of Texas, my hope is that you have as much fun using this Activity Book as I did writing it.

Enjoy your Texas Experience—it's the trip of a lifetime!!

Carole Marsh

The Texas Experience Series

The Texas Experience! Paperback Book

My First Pocket Guide to Texas!

The Big Texas Reproducible Activity Book

The Totally Texas Coloring Book!

My First Book About Texas!

Texas Jeopardy: Answers & Questions About Our State

Texas "Jography!": A Fun Run Through Our State

The Texas Experience Sticker Pack

The Texas Experience! Poster/Map

Discover Texas CD-ROM

Texas "GEO" Bingo Game

Texas "HISTO" Bingo Game

Fabulous Flag!

The Texas state flag is red, white, and blue with a white star.

Color the flag so you can see it too!

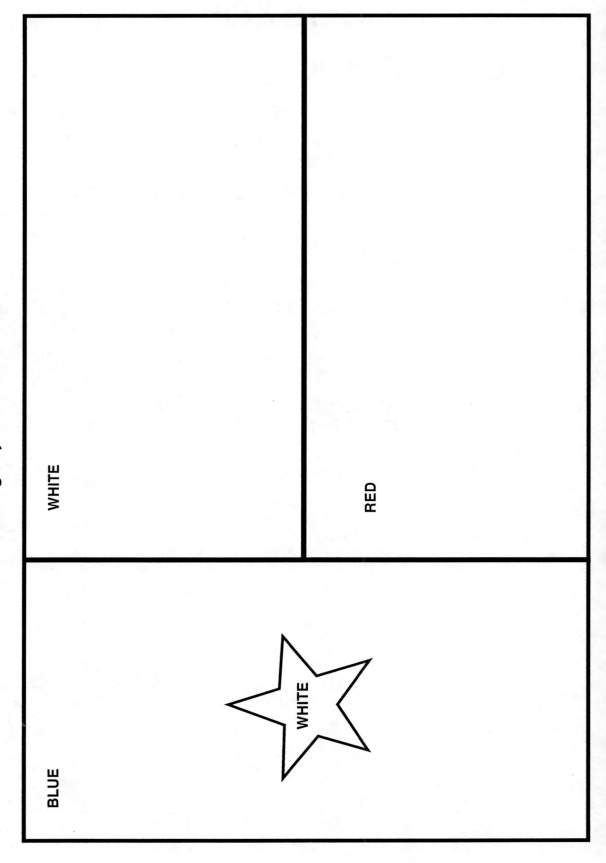

WHITE

RED

BLUE

WHITE

In The Beginning...
Came The Spanish

In 1519, Alonso Alvarez de Pineda arrived from Spain and mapped the Texas coast. In 1528, Alvar Nunez Cabeza explored Texas after a shipwreck. In 1541, Francisco Vásquez de Coronado led an expedition across western Texas.

Help these famous explorers find their way from Europe to Texas.

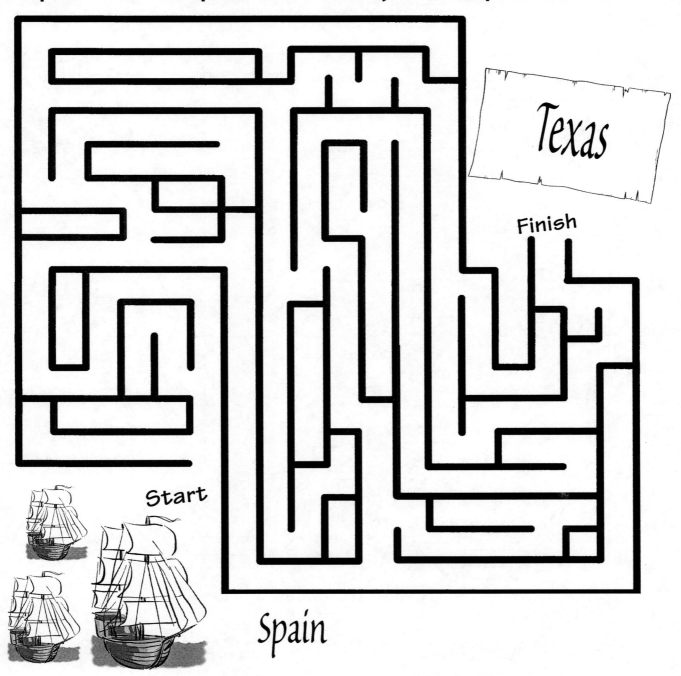

Buzzing Around Texas!

Find the answers to the questions in the maze. Write them on the lines. Follow a path through the maze in the same order as your answers to get the bee to the honey pot.

The capital of Texas is __ __ __ __ __ __.

Texas' state nickname is the __ __ __ __ __ __ __ __ __ __ __ __ __.

Texas is in __ __ __ __ __ America.

__ __ __ __ __ __ __ __ __ __ __ is the state motto.

The beautiful __ __ __ __ __ __ __ __ __ __ __ is the state flower.

Some like the yummy state dish, __ __ __ __ __, hot and spicy.

Texas is bordered by the __ __ __ __ of Mexico.

Texas' neighbor to the west is __ __ __ __ __ __ __ __ __.

Texas' most valuable natural resource is __ __ __.

The __ __ __ __ __ __ __ __ separates Texas from Oklahoma.

__ __ __ __ __ __ __ __ is the largest city in Texas.

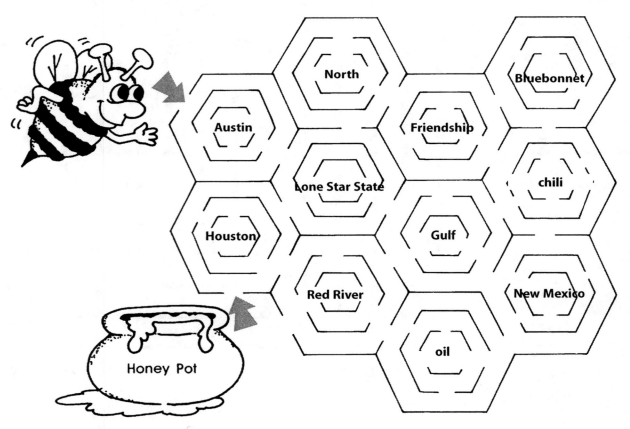

North

Bluebonnet

Austin

Friendship

Lone Star State

chili

Houston

Gulf

Red River

New Mexico

oil

Honey Pot

Spanish Ships Come Sailing!

In the 1500s, European settlers began exploring Texas. The Spanish sailed to Texas to search for cities of gold and jewels. In 1540, Francisco Vásquez de Coronado led an expedition to find the Seven Cities of Cibola and Quivira. The group wandered through western Texas and eastern New Mexico, but never found any cities of gold.

Color the ships bringing Spanish explorers looking for cities of gold.

Rhymin' Riddles

I am a state in the southwest and my name starts with a "T";
A lot of my historic sites many tourists come to see.

What am I? _____

We lived on the land of Texas before the settlers did roam;
The eastern part of Texas was our home.

Who are we? _____

We were the first European explorers looking for gold;
We came to Texas because of the stories we'd been told.

Who are we? _____

In Texas you'll find lots of us cattle;
A big herd of us would make your whole house rattle.

What are we?_____

It's an interesting tale, but true.
Today's state flag is red, white, and _____.

What am I? _____

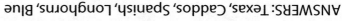
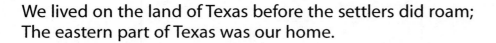

All Around Texas! Crossword Puzzle

Texas is surrounded by four states, one body of water, and a whole different country. To find out what they are, fill in the crossword using the clues below.

1. **A body of water to the east** (*across*)
2. **A state to the east** (*down*)
3. **A country to the south** (*down*)
4. **A state to the north** (*across*)
5. **A river that forms the southern border** (*across*)
6. **Another state to the east** (*across*)

N
NW   NE
W   E
SW   SE
S

Compass Rose

Texas Haystacks

Texas leads the nation in the number of farms and ranches, cattle, sheep, lambs, and goats. Many farmers grow hay to feed the animals. Below is a recipe to make your own delicious haystacks.

Make the following haystack recipe.

You will need:

1 - 8 oz. jar of peanut butter

1 - 12 oz. bag of butterscotch morsels

1 - 16 oz. can of chow mein noodles

Step 1.   Melt peanut butter together with butterscotch morsels.

Step 2.   Add chow mein noodles.

Step 3.   Drop by spoonfuls on cookie sheet and chill.

Step 4.   Enjoy!

Sing Like A Texas Bird
Word Jumble

Arrange the jumbled letters in the proper order for the names of birds found in Texas.

MOCKINGBIRD

WOODPECKER

ROBIN

BARN SWALLOW

BLUE JAY

BROWN THRASHER

CEDAR WAXWING

STARLING

WARBLER

CARDINAL

N I B O R _ _ _ _ _ _

B E U L A J Y _ _ _ _ _ _ _ _ _

N A L I C A R D _ _ _ _ _ _ _ _ _

B L E R W A R _ _ _ _ _ _ _ _

G I S L A R T N _ _ _ _ _ _ _ _

D O O W P C E E K R _ _ _ _ _ _ _ _ _ _

N B R A W L O L S W A _ _ _ _ _ _ _ _ _ _ _

D E C A R G N I W W A X _ _ _ _ _ _ _ _ _ _ _

B W O R N S H A R T H E R _ _ _ _ _ _ _ _ _ _ _ _ _

B I R D I N G M O C K _ _ _ _ _ _ _ _ _ _ _

Latin, hey?

Beautiful Butterfly!

Monarch Butterfly
Danaus Plexippus

A Monarch Butterfly has large, colorful wings and small front legs. Monarchs are brown or orange-brown, with black and white markings.

The Monarch Butterfly's wingspan is about 4 inches (10 centimeters).

Put an X by the insects that are not Monarch Butterflies and then color all the critters!

3... 2... 1... Blast Off!

Houston is home of the famous Lyndon B. Johnson Space Center. It was opened in 1964. The center is the headquarters of the U.S. manned-spaceflight program. If you visit, you can see spacecraft that have been to the moon and back, a full-scale Skylab, moon rocks, photos from Mars, and movies of spaceflights. The space center was first called the Manned Space Center, but was later renamed for President Lyndon B. Johnson.

Color the astronaut.

Don't Fence Me In

Rough and tumble cowboys have been around for a long time—working hard and living out under the stars. Their work began with roundups where cattle were marked with their owner's brand. Then the trail drive began and the cattle were driven north to be sold in Abilene. In 1866, more than a quarter of a million cattle were driven to northern cities where the cattle were sold for as much as $40 a head— a lot of money back then!

Help the cowboys drive the herd of longhorns to Abilene.

A Rough Row To Hoe!

The men and women who first came to Texas were faced with a lot of hard work to survive in the West. They travelled long distances, and worked very hard to settle the land. **Circle the things settlers would need.**

A Day In the Life Of An Explorer!

Pretend you were an explorer in the days of early Texas. You kept a diary of what you did each day. Write in the "diary" what you might have done on a hot summer day in July, 1541.

_____

_____

_____

_____

_____

_____

_____

_____

_____

_____

The Lone Star State!

Match the name of each Texas state symbol on the left with its picture on the right.

State Bird

State Insect

State Flower

State Shell

State Large
Mammal

State Small
Mammal

The First Americans

When European explorers first arrived in America, they found many Native American tribes living here. In Texas, the Apache and Comanche lived in the west, Tonkawa lived in the central region, Karankawa lived in the South, and Caddo inhabited the east. Some Native Americans used animal skins to make their homes. Others used tree branches, logs, mud, hay, and whatever else they could find!

Draw a line from the Native American tribe to the region in which they lived.

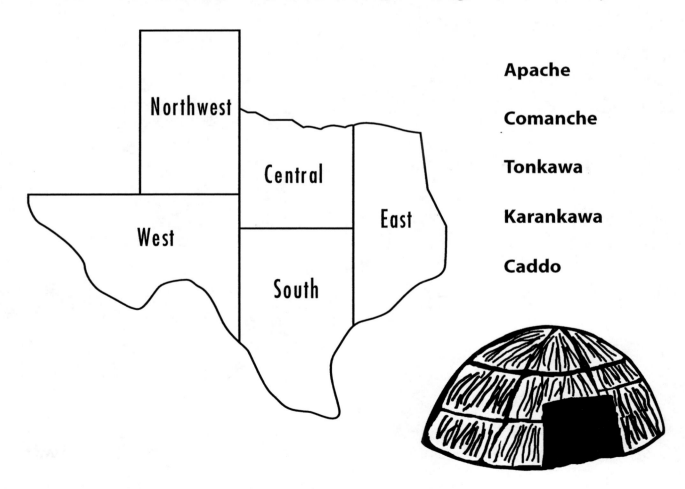

Northwest

Central

West

East

South

Apache

Comanche

Tonkawa

Karankawa

Caddo

Our Country's President

The President of the United States is our country's leader.
Do some research to complete this Presidential biography.

President's name:

_____

Paste a picture of the President here. ➤

The President was born in this state:

_____

The President lives in the

__ __ __ __ __ __   __ __ __ __ __ __ .

Members of the President's family:

_____

_____

Interesting facts about the President:

_____

_____

_____

_____

_____

_____

_____

_____

_____

Tall Tales

Tall tales are American folk stories about mostly fictional characters who were "larger than life." Some characters, like Davy Crockett and Johnny Appleseed, were actual people. The stories about them are often exaggerated, therefore the term "tall tale" is appropriate. Some characters, such as Texas' Pecos Bill, are completely fictional. As legend goes, Pecos Bill was lost as a baby and raised by coyotes. When he grew up, he became an outlaw, an Indian fighter, and finally a cowboy. On a dare, he is said to have ridden an Oklahoma cyclone. Among his many feats, Pecos Bill wrestled bears and mountain lions, dug the Rio Grande, invented the six-gun and the lasso, taught cowboys to ride broncos, and fed his own horse barbed wire. He was one tough "dude"!

Answer the questions below.

1. What are tall tales? _____

2. Name two tall tales that were actually based on the lives of real people in history! _____ and _____

3. Who raised Texas' Pecos Bill? _____

4. Name two of Pecos Bill's great feats. _____ and

   _____

5. Which cyclone (tornado) is Pecos Bill said to have ridden?_____

6. Besides Pecos Bill, list some other tall tale people you have read or heard about it.

   _____ , _____ , _____

What in the World?

A hemisphere is one-half of a sphere (globe) created by the prime meridian or equator. Every place in the world is in two hemispheres (Northern or Southern and Eastern or Western). The equator is an imaginary line that runs around the world from left to right and divides the globe into the Northern Hemisphere and Southern Hemisphere. Texas is in the Northern Hemisphere.

The prime meridian is an imaginary line that runs around the world from top to bottom and divides the globe into the Eastern Hemisphere and Western Hemisphere. Texas is in the Western Hemisphere.

Label the Eastern and Western Hemispheres.

Write PM on the prime meridian.

Color the map.

Label the Northern and Southern Hemispheres.

Write E on the equator.

Color the ocean blue.

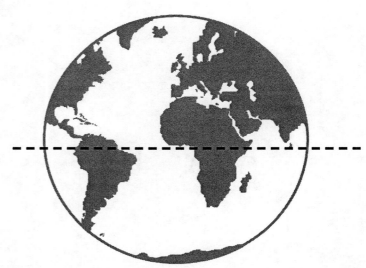

Key To A Map!

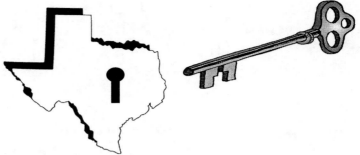

A map key, also called a map legend, shows symbols which represent different things on a map.

Match each word with a symbol for things found in the state of Texas.

airport

church

mountains

railroad

river

road

school

state capital

battle site

bird sanctuary

Something Fishy Here!

Each October, the Seafare Festival is held in Rockport, Texas. There's plenty of seafood, a gumbo cook-off, music, arts and crafts, and an "Anything that floats" boat race. There's something fishy about the picture below—part of it is missing.

Draw what is going on above the water line (a boat, fishermen, etc.) and add some other underwater fish friends.

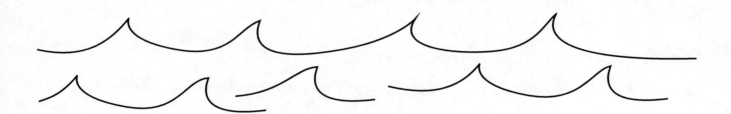

Major Minorities

Texas was important in the civil rights movement. James Farmer, born in Marshall, Texas was a civil rights leader who founded the Congress of Racial Equality (CORE).

Dr. Martin Luther King, Jr. was one of the most famous civil rights leaders. He wanted all Americans to live freely anywhere, and not just in segregated neighborhoods. Dr. King had a dream. His dream was equal rights for all Americans. He worked very hard to make all Americans "free at last." In Houston, a 26 foot tall steel sculpture by Barnett Newman called *The Broken Obelisk* was dedicated to Martin Luther King, Jr.

Many other African-Americans and Hispanic-Americans made significant contributions to for the state of Texas, the nation, and in some cases, the world. Below are a few.

Match the person to their accomplishment.

_____ 1. Carol Moseley Braun

_____ 2. John H. Johnson

_____ 3. Henry G. Cisneros

_____ 4. Mae Jemison

_____ 5. Earl Campbell

_____ 6. James Farmer

_____ 7. Barbara C. Jordan

_____ 8. Andrew "Rube" Foster

A. first African-American woman elected to the U.S. Senate

B. played for the University of Texas and the Houston Oilers; Heisman trophy winner

C. first African-American woman in space

D. founded Congress Of Racial Equality

E. founded successful African-American publishing company

F. Hispanic leader; served as cabinet member for President Clinton

G. first African-American woman from the south to serve in the U.S. Congress

H. African-American ballplayer who organized the National Negro League

ANSWERS: 1.A, 2.E, 3.H, 4.C, 5.B, 6.D, 7.G, 8.H

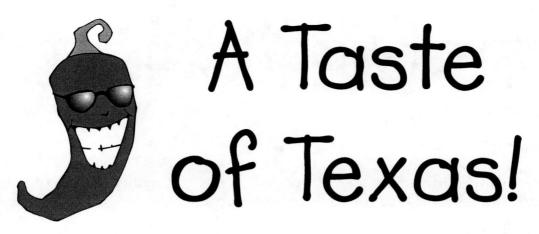

A Taste of Texas!

Texas cuisine (food) has been referred to as "Tex-Mex" because of the many influences of the Mexican food culture. However, Texas' unique food has also been flavored by Eastern, Midwestern, and Southern cooking. Texas is known for its chili, barbecue and peppers. Many Texans like these foods HOT! HOT! HOT!
The word "chile" refers to the peppers. Technically, chile is a fruit. It has high doses of vitamins C and A. Texas, along with other Southwestern states, has chile-eating contests. The rules are simple: eat hot, hotter, hottest chiles with a straight face. Points are taken off if the contestants flinch, fan, cringe, or breathe heavily after eating the chile.

Many Texans know how to remedy a "chile hot mouth". But it's not what you think - don't reach for a glass of water!

To find out what you should eat or drink to remedy the situation, cross out every other letter below. The letters that are left will give you the answers. Write them in the spaces below.

m w i e l r k a y s o d g z u x r v t b p n e m a l n g u h t q b w u v t d t m e v r q

_ _ _ _ _ ,   _ _ _ _ _ _ _ _ , and _ _ _ _ _ _ _   _ _ _ _ _ _ _

Map of North America

This is a map of North America.

Color the state of Texas red.

Color the rest of the United States yellow. (Alaska and Hawaii are part of the United States and should also be colored yellow.)

Color Canada green.

Color Mexico blue.

A River Runs Through It!

The state of Texas is blessed with many rivers. See if you can wade right in and figure out which river name completes the sentences below!

1. The __ __ __ __ __ __ __ __ __ __ means "big river" in Spanish.

2. The __ __ __ __ __ __ River separates Texas from Louisiana.

3. The __ __ __ River helps form the border between Oklahoma and Texas.

4. The __ __ __ __ __ __ __ __ __ __ River has the same name as the town famous for the Alamo.

5. The __ __ __ __ __ __ __ __ River is named for another state. (The home of the "Rockies" professional baseball team.)

6. The __ __ __ __ __ __ __ __ River sounds like it is from Canada but runs through northern Texas.

7. The __ __ __ __ __ __ __ __ __ __ River has the same name as one of Texas' national parks.

8. Washington-on-the-Brazos is a town on the __ __ __ __ __ __ River.

9. The __ __ __ __ __ __ River sounds like a nice river.

10. Red, __ __ __ __ __, and blue are the colors in the U.S. flag and the Texas flag. (The missing color is also the name of a Texas river!)

ANSWERS: 1. Rio Grande, 2. Sabine, 3. Red, 4. San Antonio, 5. Colorado, 6. Canadian, 7. Guadalupe, 8. Brazos, 9. Nueces, 10. White

Remember The Alamo!

In 1836, Texans were fighting for their independence from Mexico. In February, a Mexican army led by General Santa Anna marched into San Antonio and surrounded the old walled mission called the Alamo. Inside, there were 189 defenders including Jim Bowie, Davy Crockett, and William Travis. According to legend, Travis called the Alamo defenders into a group, drew a line in the dirt with his sword, and announced that all who wished to fight should take one step forward. Bravely knowing their fate was sealed, all but one of the 189 took that step. The Mexican army of thousands greatly outnumbered the Alamo defenders. After a fierce attack that lasted 13 days, the Mexican soldiers killed all of the Alamo defenders.

Color the Alamo.

Our State's Rules

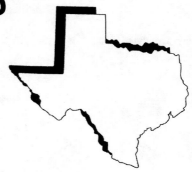

Use the code to complete the sentences.

A	B	C	D	E	F	G	H	I	J	K	L	M	N	O	P	Q	R	S	T
1	2	3	4	5	6	7	8	9	10	11	12	13	14	15	16	17	18	19	20

U	V	W	X	Y	Z
21	22	23	24	25	26

1. State rules are called ___ ___ ___ ___.
   12   1   23   19

2. Laws are made in our state ___ ___ ___ ___ ___ ___ ___.
   3   1   16   9   20   1   12

3. The leader of our state is the ___ ___ ___ ___ ___ ___ ___ ___.
   7   15   22   5   18   14   15   18

4. We live in the state of ___ ___ ___ ___ ___.
   20   5   24   1   19

5. The capital of our state is ___ ___ ___ ___ ___ ___.
   1   21   19   20   9   14

ANSWERS: 1. laws 2. capital 3. governor 4. Texas 5. Austin

What Founding Father Am I?

From the Word Bank, find my name and fill in the blank. (My name might be used twice.)

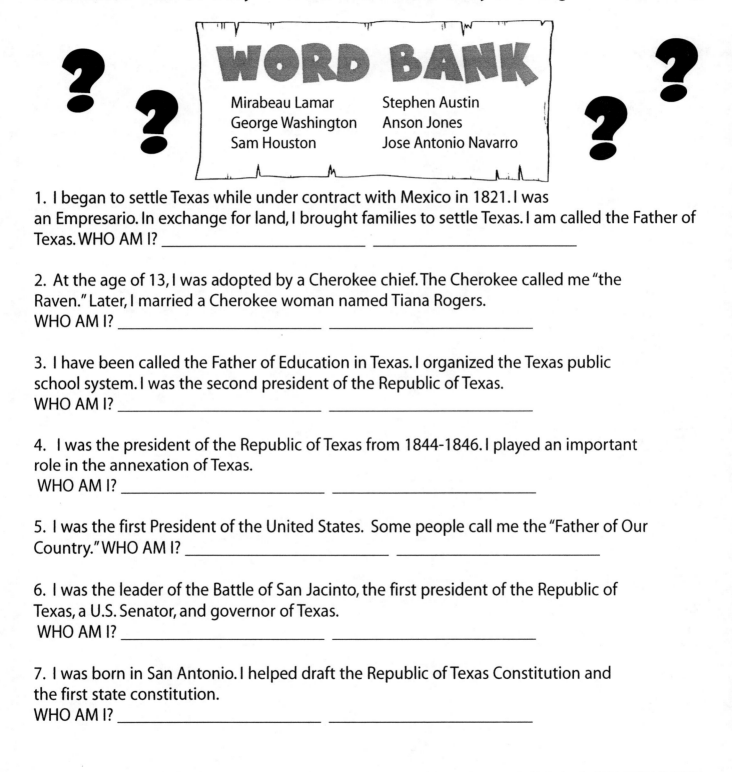

WORD BANK

Mirabeau Lamar   Stephen Austin
George Washington   Anson Jones
Sam Houston   Jose Antonio Navarro

1. I began to settle Texas while under contract with Mexico in 1821. I was an Empresario. In exchange for land, I brought families to settle Texas. I am called the Father of Texas. WHO AM I? _____ _____

2. At the age of 13, I was adopted by a Cherokee chief. The Cherokee called me "the Raven." Later, I married a Cherokee woman named Tiana Rogers.
WHO AM I? _____ _____

3. I have been called the Father of Education in Texas. I organized the Texas public school system. I was the second president of the Republic of Texas.
WHO AM I? _____ _____

4. I was the president of the Republic of Texas from 1844-1846. I played an important role in the annexation of Texas.
 WHO AM I? _____ _____

5. I was the first President of the United States. Some people call me the "Father of Our Country." WHO AM I? _____ _____

6. I was the leader of the Battle of San Jacinto, the first president of the Republic of Texas, a U.S. Senator, and governor of Texas.
 WHO AM I? _____ _____

7. I was born in San Antonio. I helped draft the Republic of Texas Constitution and the first state constitution.
WHO AM I? _____ _____

ANSWERS: 1. Stephen Austin, 2. Sam Houston, 3. Mirabeau Lamar, 4. Anson Jones, 5. George Washington, 6. Samuel Houston, 7. Jose Antonio Navarro.

Crazy Quilt!

Quilts made by Texans have become valuable heirlooms. Heirlooms are family possessions handed down from generation to generation. Often, a woman would tell a story with the pattern of her quilt. Draw some designs that tell a story about you, then color the quilt below. Write a story about the design.

Write your story about the design of your quilt here.

_____

_____

_____

_____

_____

_____

_____

The Rio Grande!

The Spanish gave the Rio Grande its name. In Spanish, the words *Rio Grande* mean "big river". Antonio de Espejo, a Spanish explorer, called it the River of the North. The Rio Grande is the longest river in Texas. According to the International Boundary and Water Commission, the river is 1,896 miles (3,034 kilometers) long. The river forms the boundary of Texas and the international U.S.–Mexican boundary. On most Mexican maps, the river is called Río Bravo. Sometimes the river changes its course, and the boundary moves. Ysleta, the oldest city in Texas, was once on the other side of the river! San Elizario is another one of the oldest towns in Texas. It also lies in the Rio Grande Valley. The U.S. and Mexico worked together to build the Amistad Dam on the Rio Grande. As the river travels, it moves faster and picks up and carries sand, mud, and pebbles. This is deposited as silt along the lower banks and in the mouth of the river. The river ends in the Gulf of Mexico.

Use words from the passage above to fill in the blanks below.

1. *Rio Grande* means big _____.   R __ __ __ __
2. Kind of border between Texas and Mexico.   I __ __ __ __ __ __ __ __ __ __ __ __ __
3. Ysleta is the … city in Texas.   O __ __ __ __ __ __

4. The river ends in the … of Mexico.   G __ __ __
5. Name on Mexican maps: … Bravo.   R __ __ __
6. Spanish explorer … de Espejo.   A __ __ __ __ __ __ __
7. "The River of the …"   N __ __ __ __
8. Amistad … was built by the U.S. and Mexico.   D __ __
9. San … is in the Rio Grande valley.   E __ __ __ __ __ __ __

Texas Wheel of Fortune, Indian Style!

The names of Texas' many Native American tribes are in the puzzles below. Let's play Wheel of Fortune!

See if you can figure out the Wheel of Fortune-style puzzles below! "Vanna" has given you a few letters in each word to help you out!

C _ _ D D _

_ R K K _ S _

_ T T _ C _ P _

B _ D A _ _

D _ _ D _ S E

_ P _ C H _

C _ _ A N C H _

ANSWERS: CADDO, ARKOKISA, ATTACAPA, BIDAI, DEADOSE, APACHE, COMANCHE

We're On A Mission!

Some of North America's oldest buildings survive in Texas, built by Spanish missionaries who wanted to educate and civilize the local natives. Spanish missions established in the 1700s are evidence of early efforts to colonize the region and spread the Catholic faith throughout the local Native American communities. San Antonio is the "Mission Heartland of Texas" today. It's home to 4 separate missions–5 if you include The Alamo.

Take a tour of the San Antonio Missions Trail and see if you can match the mission with its description on the left. Write the number in the space provided and check your answers below!

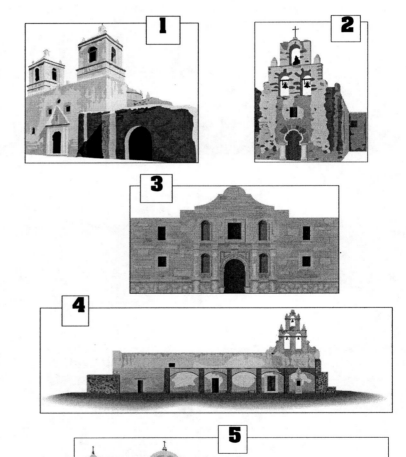

Mission Concepcion is known for its handsome twin towers.

_____

The Alamo is where Davy Crockett, Jim Bowie, William Travis, and more than 180 other defenders were killed by General Santa Anna and his Mexican army in the Texas War of Independence.

_____

Mission San Juan has a distinctive 3-bell tower.

_____

Mission Espada also has a 3-bell tower and has a keyhole-shaped door.

_____

Mission San Jose is dubbed "Queen of the Missions" and is considered by some to be the most beautiful mission.

_____

ANSWERS: 1. Mission Concepcion 2. Mission Espada 3. The Alamo 4. Mission San Juan 5. Mission San Jose

It Could Happen— And It Did!

These historical events from Texas' past are all out of whack.

Can you put them back together in the correct order?
(There's a great big hint at the end of each sentence.)

• Caddo Confederacy forms civilization based on agriculture (1400)
• Texas wins independence from Mexico (1836)
• Texas adopts present state constitution (1876)
• Spaniards establish first mission settlement at Ysleta, near El Paso (1682)
• Stephen F. Austin begins to settle Texas under agreement with
  Mexican government (1821)
• Texas secedes from Union–joins Confederate States of America (1861)
• Texas readmitted to the Union (1870)
• Texas officially joins the Union as the 28th state (1845)
• Texas Revolution begins (1835)
• Mission San Antonio de Valero, later known as the Alamo, was founded (1718)

1. _____

2. _____

3. _____

4. _____

5. _____

6. _____

7. _____

8. _____

9. _____

10. _____

 # Two Make One

See if you can figure out the two words that make up the compound word.

Write the two words on the lines below the big one.

1

GRAPEFRUIT	BUTTERFLY	LONGHORN
_____ _____	_____ _____	_____ _____
SONGBIRD	SIDEOATS	PALMWOOD
_____ _____	_____ _____	_____ _____
RAILROAD	SOUTHWEST	PANHANDLE
_____ _____	_____ _____	_____ _____
SHIPWRECK	NEWSPAPER	OUTLAWS
_____ _____	_____ _____	_____ _____
CHAMPIONSHIP	SEASHORE	CHUCKWAGON
_____ _____	_____ _____	_____ _____
WESTWARD	LONESOME	COWBOY
_____ _____	_____ _____	_____ _____
FOOTBALL	COWGIRL	RAGTIME
_____ _____	_____ _____	_____ _____

ANSWERS: 1. Grape Fruit 2. Butter Fly 3. Long Horn 4. Song Bird 5. Side Oats 6. Palm Wood 7. Rail Road 8. South West 9. Pan Handle 10. Ship Wreck 11. News Paper 12. Out Laws 13. Champion Shi 14. Sea Shore 15. Chuck Wago 16. West Ward 17. Lone Some 18. Cow Boy 19. Foot Ball 20. Cow Girl 21. Rag Time

HOWLING HURRICANES

Word Search

A hurricane is a violent storm with wind speeds more than 74 miles per hour.

Find the names of hurricanes that have blown through the coast of Texas.

Alicia	**Bret**	**Gilbert**	**Chantal**
Allen	**Carla**	**"The Storm"**	
Audrey	**Celia**	**Beulah**	

```
B E U L A H G X
C A R L A Z I X
H O A I C I L A
A L L E N I B P
N O O O B R E T
T H E S T O R M
A U D R E Y T Z
L O O C E L I A
```

Top Ten Towns!

Here's a list of the ten largest cities by population in Texas.

Put them in the correct order (starting with the largest as #1). There's a hint with each city.

Austin (5)   1._____

Fort Worth (6)   2._____

Lubbock (9)   3._____

Houston (#1 - largest)   4._____

San Antonio (2)   5._____

Garland (#10)   6._____

Dallas (3)   7._____

El Paso (4)   8._____

Arlington (7)   9._____

Corpus Christi (8)   10._____

Can you guess which Texas city this is?

_____

Here's a hint—it's really big and has lots and lots of people!

Texas Writers

Fill in the missing first or last name of these famous Texas writers.

1. First name: Dobie J.
   Last name: _____

2. First name: _____
   Last name: McMurtry

3. First name: Katherine Anne
   Last name: _____

4. First name: _____
   Last name: Castaneda

5. First name: Walter Prescott
   Last name: _____

6. First name: _____
   Last name: Owens

7. First name: Andy
   Last name: _____ _____

To be a reader or not to be a reader — there's only one answer!

Answers: 1.Frank 2.Larry 3.Porter 4.Carlos E. 5.Webb 6.William 7.Adams

Flags Flying– Then and Now

Many different flags have flown over Texas over the past 300 years. Here are just a few.

Color each flag and imagine for a moment how it might have looked waving in the Texas breeze.

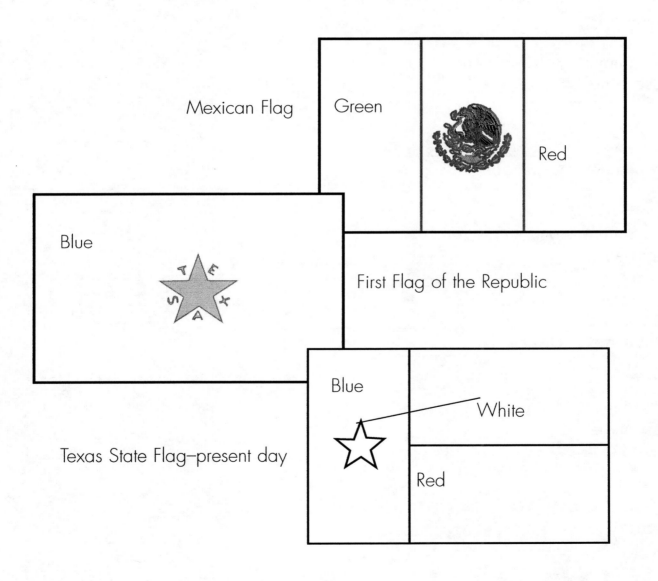

Mexican Flag — Green — Red

First Flag of the Republic — Blue

Texas State Flag–present day — Blue — White — Red

Texas' Venomous Snakes!

Four species of venomous (poisonous) snakes live in Texas. Using the alphabet code, see if you can find out their names.

Use the code to complete the sentences.

A	B	C	D	E	F	G	H	I	J	K	L	M	N	O	P	Q	R	S	T
1	2	3	4	5	6	7	8	9	10	11	12	13	14	15	16	17	18	19	20

U	V	W	X	Y	Z
21	22	23	24	25	26

___ ___ ___ ___ ___ ___ ___   ___ ___ ___ ___ ___ ___ ___ ___ ___ ___ ___
23 5 19 20 5 18 14   18 1 20 20 12 5 19 14 1 11 5

___ ___ ___ ___ ___ ___ ___ ___ ___
3 15 16 16 5 18 8 5 1 4

___ ___ ___ ___ ___ ___ ___ ___ ___ ___
3 15 18 1 12   19 14 1 11 5

___ ___ ___ ___ ___ ___ ___ ___ ___ ___ ___
3 15 20 20 15 14 13 15 21 20 8

___ ___ ___ ___ ___ ___ ___ ___ ___ ___ ___ ___ ___
3 1 20 5 25 5 4   19 14 1 11 5

ANSWERS: Western Rattlesnake, Copperhead, Coral Snake, Cottonmouth, Cat-Eyed Snake

Texas Through the Times

Many great things have happened in Texas throughout its history, both past and present. Chronicle the following important Texas events by solving math problems to find out the years in which they happened.

1. Alonso Álvarez de Pineda
   maps Texas Coast   2-1=   5x1=   2-1=   3x3=

2. Álvar Núnez Cabeza de Vaca
   explores Texas   6-5=   1x5=   0+2=   16÷2=

3. Coronado leads expedition
   across Western Texas   5-4=   7-2=   9-5=   0+1=

4. Mission San Antonio de Valero
   (The Alamo!) is founded   7-6=   3+4=   10-9=   4x2=

5. Texas wins independence
   from Mexico   9-8=   2x4=   6-3=   2x3=

6. Texas joins the Union as the
   28th state   3-2=   1x8=   2x2=   6-1=

7. First big oil strike
   at Spindletop   1x1=   10-1=   7x0=   1x1=

8. Eisenhower becomes first
   Texas born president   9-8=   3x3=   4+1=   9÷3=

9. Kennedy assassinated in Dallas;
   Lyndon Johnson becomes president   7-6=   3+6=   3x2=   8-5=

10. George Bush elected president   1+0=   8+1=   3+5=   4x2=

ANSWERS: 1.1519 2.1528 3.1541 4.1718 5.1836 6.1845 7.1901 8.1953 9.1963 10.1988

Texas Native Americans!

Native Americans were the first people living in Texas before the explorers and settlers came.

Circle the things that Native Americans might have used in their everyday life.

Texas Word Wheel- Give It A Spin

The words on the wheel (clockwise from top):

Zaharias, Austin, Bluebonnet, Central, Davy Crockett, Eisenhower, Four, Guadalupe Bass, Houston, Inks Lake State Park, Jefferson, Kickapoo, Lone Star, Mavericks, Native American, Oil, Pecos Bill, Quarter Horse, Rio Grande, Sam Houston, Texas Revolution, Union, Valley Nature Center, Washington, X Bar Ranch, Yellow Rose of Texas

Center: Texas **WORD** Wheel

From the Word Wheel of Texas' names and things, answer the following questions.

The first president of the United States was George __ __ __ __ __ __ __ __ __ __.

Texas' nickname is the __ __ __ __ __ __ __ __ State.

Texas can be divided into __ __ __ __ natural regions.

The __ __ __ __ __ __ __ Lowland occupies much of north-central Texas.

The largest river in Texas is the __ __ __ __ __ __ __ __ __.

__ __ __ __ __ __ is the capital city.

Texas' most valuable natural resource is __ __ __.

Texas officially joined the __ __ __ __ __ as the 28th state in 1845.

Dwight D. __ __ __ __ __ __ __ __ __ __ was the first Texas-born President of the United States.

Sam __ __ __ __ __ __ __ was the first President of the Republic of Texas.

The Texas state flower is the __ __ __ __ __ __ __ __ __ __.

Texans Love Salsa!

Salsa is a popular Mexican dish. Due to the Mexican influence on Texan cuisine, salsa is also a favorite in the Lone Star State!

Ask an adult to help you make this easy (and yummy!) salsa recipe below. Grab ahold of a bag of tortilla chips, amigo, and enjoy this Tex-Mex Salsa!

Tex-Mex Salsa

Ingredients:
- 2 cans whole, peeled tomatoes
- 4 fresh jalapeños
- 1 medium onion
- 1 clove of garlic

Directions:
1. seed jalapeños
2. chop up all ingredients; stir together
3. serve with chips and enjoy

Mmmmmm! When you're hot, you're hot!

Spanish Explorers

In 1492, Christopher Columbus was sent by the king and queen of Spain to find a western sea route to Asia. He discovered the "New World" which we now call America. In 1521, Juan Ponce de Leon, another Spanish explorer, set out from Puerto Rico to discover riches and conquer land. In 1519, Alonso Álvarez de Piñeda mapped the Texas Gulf Coast. Later, other Spanish explorers, including Cabeza and Coronado, came to Texas and other parts of what we now call the United States. Color the map.

Texas State Seal

The state seal has a five pointed star with a live oak branch and an olive branch.

Color the state seal.

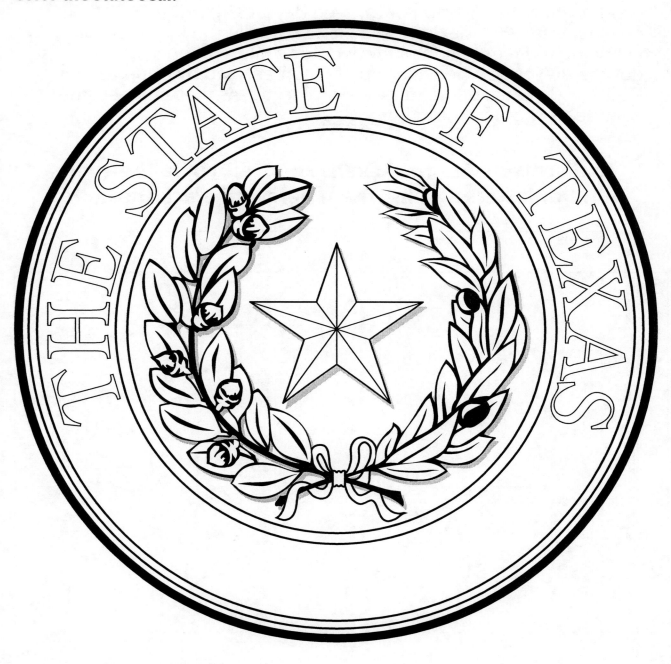

The Alamo

Texas fought for its independence from Mexico and became a republic. One of the most famous battles of the Texas Revolution was fought at the Alamo. For thirteen days, 189 patriots held their own against 4,000 Mexican soldiers. Eventually, the Mexicans killed everyone there except for a few women, children, and slaves. Texans got their revenge when a group of volunteers led by General Sam Houston defeated Santa Anna at San Jacinto. As they charged, the volunteers shouted something...

To discover what the Texans shouted, circle the even number letters and list them below to crack the code.

_ _ _ _ _ _ _ _ _ _   _ _ _   _ _ _ _ _ _ !

1	2	3	4	5	6	7
L	R	I	E	N	M	C
8	**9**	**10**	**11**	**12**	**13**	**14**
E	O	M	L	B	N	E
15	**16**	**17**	**18**	**19**	**20**	**21**
W	R	A	T	S	H	T
22	**23**	**24**	**25**	**26**	**27**	**28**
E	H	A	E	L	P	A
29	**30**	**31**	**32**	**33**	**34**	**35**
R	M	E	O	S	!	I

"Little" Mermaid

West Indian manatees are gentle, slow-moving sea mammals. Homesick sailors would often mistake them for mermaids because their flippers looked like little hands! The Texas Parks and Wildlife Department has declared the manatee in danger of becoming extinct in the state of Texas. Almost half of all manatee deaths are caused by humans and boat propeller blades.

Help the manatee find the warm safe waters.

START

WARM
SAFE
WATERS

American Alligator Dot-To-Dot

In the marshy bayous of East Texas some 200,000 alligators live. They are Texas' largest reptile and feed on fish and other small animals, but seldom attack humans. Ready for a swim?

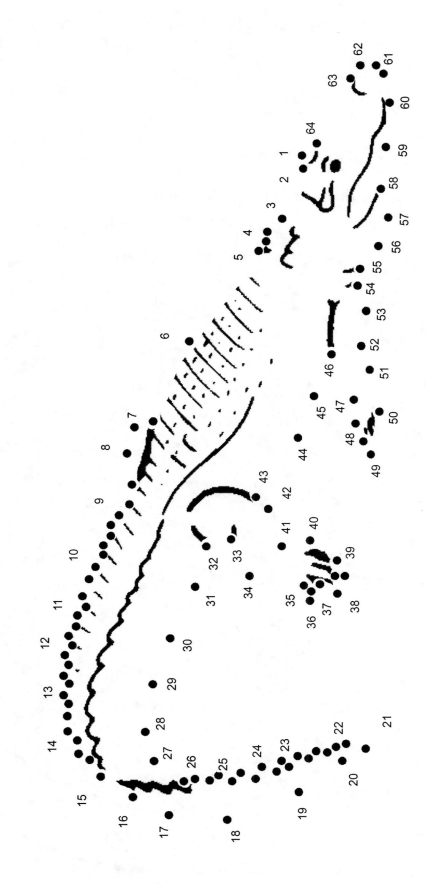

Similar Symbols

Texas has many symbols including a state bird, plant, large mammal, insect, and small mammal. Circle the item in each row that is not a symbol of Texas.

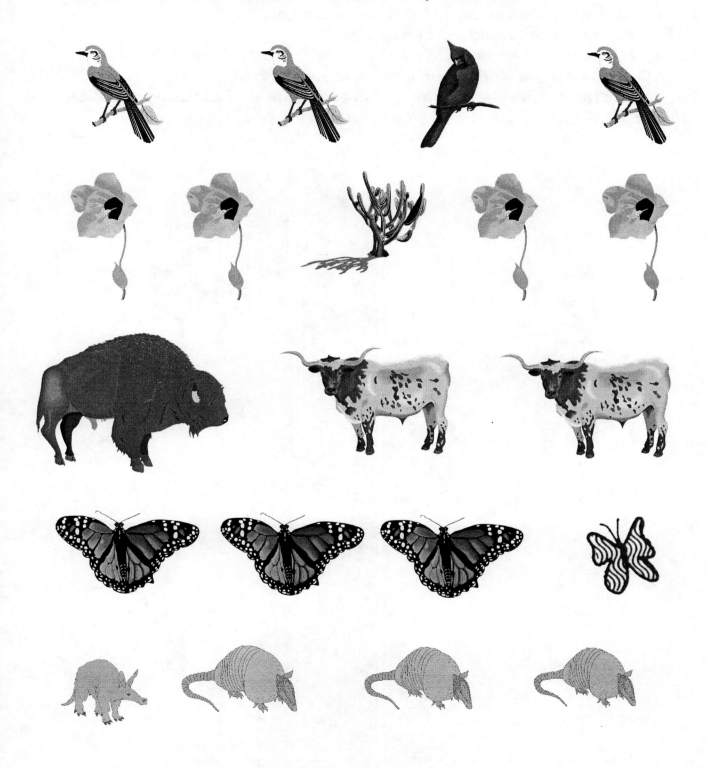

People and Their Jobs!

Can you identify these people and their jobs?

Put an A by the person involved in law enforcement.
Put a B by the people working at an oil rig.
Put a C by the person working at a federal government office in Austin.
Put a D by the person working on a ranch in south Texas.
Put an E by the person working for a high-tech computer company in Dallas.
Put an F by the person that works on a boat on the Gulf of Mexico.

Ginny of Corpus Christi

 lives in . lives in Corpus Christi in the Gulf Coast Region

near the . She likes to on the and pick

up . Her favorite thing to do is . She puts on her

and . The weather is usually but some days it can be

Ginny's mother is a at a in Corpus Christi, and her father is

a . On Saturday, her family had a  . Ginny's favorite food was .

For dessert, she ate an . Her family drove in their 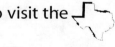 to Shoreline

Boulevard to visit the State Aquarium. They saw exhibits of more than 250

species of in over 350,000 gallons of sea water in many different marine

habitats. and her and had a wonderful time at the Aquarium.

 loves living in near the  .

The Scenic Route

Imagine that you are leading a tour of famous Texas cities and landmarks. Circle the places below on the map, then number them in the order which you would visit them, east to west.

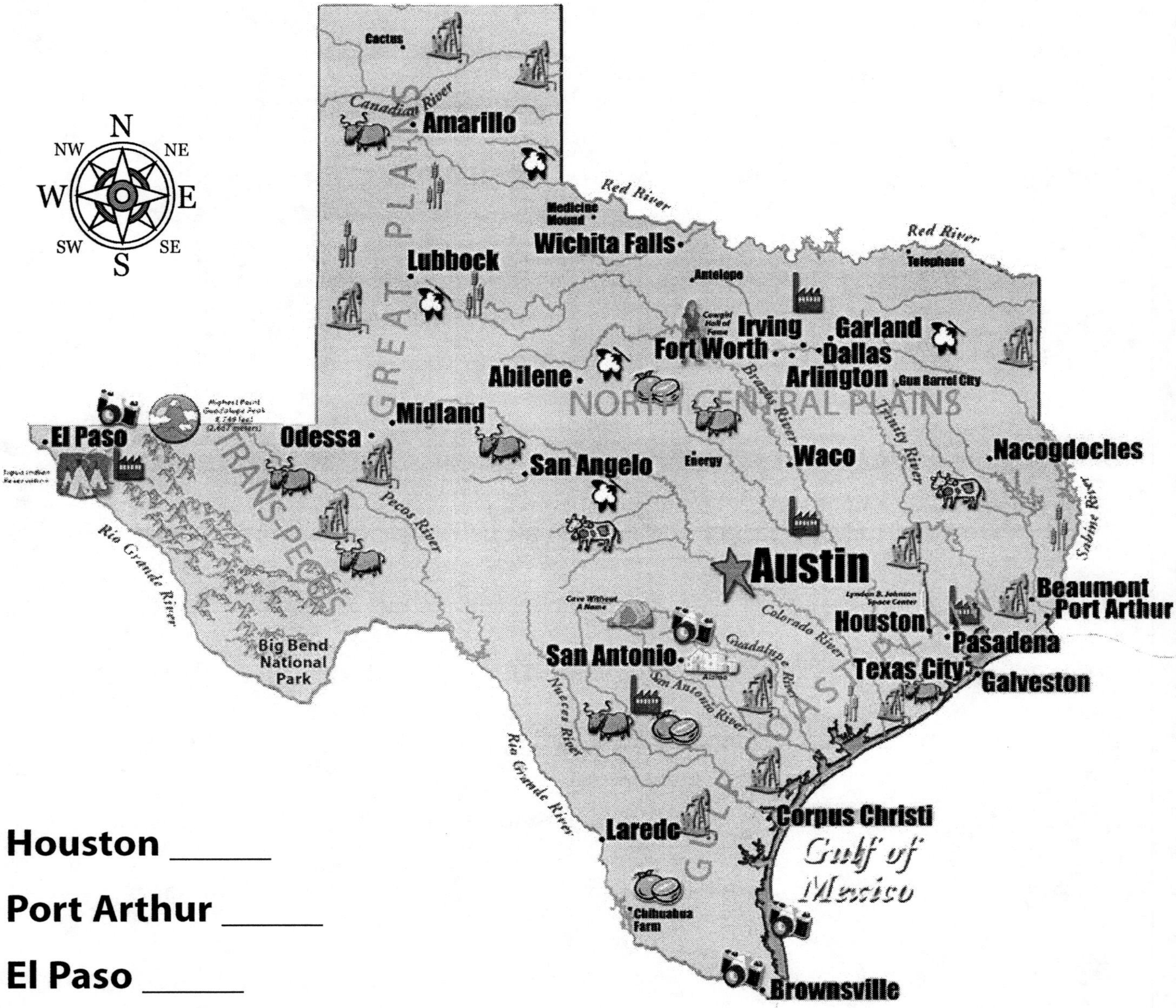

Houston _____

Port Arthur _____

El Paso _____

Lubbock _____

Big Bend National Park _____

San Antonio _____

Texas is a great state!

ANSWERS: 1. Port Arthur, 2. Houston, 3. San Antonio, 4. Lubbock, 5. Big Bend National Park, 6. El Paso

Texas Word Wheel – Give It Another Spin

From the Word Wheel of Texas names and things, answer the following questions.

1. _____ is the island city that was devastated by "The Storm" in 1900.

2. Tall tales tell about the mythical _____ _____ who was raised by coyotes.

3. The _____ Indians roam freely between Texas and Mexico.

4. The Texas state small mammal is the _____.

5. General _____ _____ led the charge at San Jacinto against Santa Anna and the Mexican army shouting, "Remember the Alamo!".

6. Babe Didrickson _____ was an accomplished female athlete from Port Arthur.

7. _____ is the home of the Dallas Cowboys.

8. William B. _____ commanded Texas forces at the Alamo.

ANSWERS: 1. Galveston, 2. Pecos Bill, 3. Kickapoo, 4. armadillo, 5. Sam Houston, 6. Zaharias, 7. Irving, 8. Travis.

Texas Talk

In Texas, people have their own way of "saying things." These terms are called "colloquial sayings," which means an informal way of saying something. So, "saddle up" and match the colloquial sayings below with their meanings, pardner!

1. You're a sight for sore eyes
2. Many fish to fry
3. A dead bee can still sting
4. Her phone's off the hook
5. Like trying to bag flies
6. It wouldn't cut hot butter
7. She rustled up some grub
8. He is about to blow a gasket
9. In high cotton
10. Bright as a new penny

A. crazy
B. caution
C. dull
D. good-looking
E. busy
F. difficult
G. rich
H. food
I. mad
J. smart

SMART
CRAZY
DULL
BUSY
Rich
MAD

Slavery In Texas:
Nothing To Be Proud Of

Southern immigrants to Texas began bringing their slaves with them in 1820, but the southern plantation system for raising crops hadn't reached farther than eastern Texas when the Civil War began in 1861. On June 19, 1865, Union soldiers read the Emancipation Proclamation to Texan slaves. The proclamation was two years old, but it was the first time they had been allowed to hear it. African-American Texans commemorate this event today with a celebration called Juneteenth.

Help the slave escape by using the code to decipher the message.

Key: 1=A, 2=B, 3=C, 5=E, 8=H, 9=I, 13=M, 14=N, 15=O, 16=P, 18=R, 19=S, 20=T

13-5-5-20 9-14 20-8-5 2-1-18-14

20-15 5-19-3-1-16-5.

Famous Texas People Scavenger Hunt

Here is a list of just some of the famous people from our state. Go on a scavenger hunt to see if you can "capture" a fact about each one. Use an encyclopedia, almanac, or other resource you might need. Happy hunting!

FAMOUS PERSON   **FAMOUS FACT**

Stephen F. Austin

Sam Houston

Bill Pickett

James Farmer

Barbara Jordan

Huddie Ledbetter

Scott Joplin

Nolan Ryan

Dobie J. Frank

Elizabet Ney

Chester W. Nimitz

Audie Murphy

Gail Borden

Ferid Murid

James S. Hogg

Sam Rayburn

Henry G. Cisneros

Lyndon B. Johnson

Dwight D. Eisenhower

Sandra Day O'Conner

Sea Creatures

What is this scary predator lurking under the water of Texas' gulf shore? Just when you wanted to take a swim! Actually, sharks help maintain a balance in the underwater world of the Gulf of Mexico. They eat injured, weak, and sick fish which helps prevent the spread of disease.

 Color these spaces brown.   **Color these spaces blue.**

 Color these spaces green.

Looking For

Match the things on the left with a home on the right!

1. **Lightning Whelk**

2. **Spicy hot bowl of chili**

3. **Flying Watermelon Seeds**

4. **Buddy Holly**

5. **"Free" 72-oz. Steak**

6. **Dwight D. Eisenhower**

7. **Unhappy Rattlesnake**

8. **Kickapoos**

9. **Alonso Alvarez de Pineda**

10. **First Big Oil Strike**

A. **Spindletop (near Beaumont)**

B. **Denison**

C. **World's Championship Chili Cook-off**

D. **Gulf Coast shore**

E. **Rattlesnake Roundup (Sweetwater)**

F. **The Great Watermelon Thump (Luling)**

G. **Eagle Pass in south Texas**

H. **The Big Texas Steak Ranch (Amarillo)**

I. **Coast of Texas in 1519**

J. **Lubbock**

ANSWERS: 1.D, 2.C, 3.F, 4.J, 5.H, 6.B, 7.E, 8.G, 9.I, 10.A

Texas People

A state is not just towns and mountains and rivers. A state is its people! The really important people in a state are not always famous. You may know them—they may be your mom, your dad, or your teacher. The average, everyday person is the one who makes the state a good state. How? By working hard, by paying taxes, by voting, and by helping Texas children grow up to be good state citizens!

Match each Texas person with their accomplishment.

1. Gene Autrey

2. Earl Campbell

3. Dwight Eisenhower

4. Oveta Hobby

5. Buddy Holly

6. Scott Joplin

7. Katherine Porter

8. Chester Nimitz

9. Babe Zaharias

A. Olympic track and field gold medalist

B. commander of the Pacific Fleet during World War II

C. writer, Pulitzer Prize winner

D. social reformer, publisher

E. singer, musician

F. singer, actor, baseball team owner

G. pro football player

H. 34th U.S. president

I. musician, founder of ragtime

Answers: 1–F; 2–G; 3–H; 4–D; 5–E; 6–I; 7–C; 8–B; 9–A

Gazetteer

A gazetteer is a list of places. Use the word bank to complete the names of some of these famous places in our state:

1. D__L __A__

2. SA __ AN__ __NIO

3. F__R__ W__ __TH

4. R__ __ GR __N__E

5. HO__S__ __N

6. CHI__ __A__UAN D__S__RT

7. B__G __E N__

8. T__E __LAM__

9. TH __ P__ __HA__ __LE

10. __U__ __ O__ M__X I__O

Word Bank

The Alamo
Houston
Chihuahuan
Desert
Fort Worth
Rio Grande
The Panhandle
Big Bend
San Antonio
Gulf of Mexico
Dallas

How Many People In Texas?

STATE OF TEXAS
CENSUS REPORT

Every 10 years, it's time for Texans to stand up and be counted. Since 1790, the United States has conducted a census, or count, of each of its citizens. Practice filling out a census form.

Name _____ Age [ ]

Place of Birth _____

Current Address _____

Does your family own or rent where you live? _____

How long have you lived in Texas? _____

How many people are in your family? _____

How many females? [ ]   How many males? [ ]

What are their ages? _____

How many rooms are in your house? [ ]

How is your home heated? _____

How many cars does your family own? [ ]

How many telephones in your home? [ ]

Is your home a farm? _____

Sounds pretty nosy, doesn't it? But a census is very important. The information is used for all kinds of purposes, including setting budgets, zoning land, determining how many schools to build, and much more. The census helps Texas leaders plan for the future needs of its citizens. Hey, that's you!!

Davy Crockett, King Of The Wild Frontier

Davy Crockett was born in 1786 in eastern Tennessee. As a young man, he was a farmer and helped trail cattle to Virginia. Crockett also served in the Creek War (1813-1814) under General Andrew Jackson. He entered the political arena in 1821. After serving Tennessee as a statesman, Crockett was elected to the U.S. Congress and spent 2 terms in Washington, D.C. After losing an election in 1835, he headed to Texas. Crockett led a band of volunteers to help Texans fight for their independence from Mexico. On March 6, 1836, Davy Crockett and more than 180 men were killed by the Mexican Army at the Alamo in San Antonio.

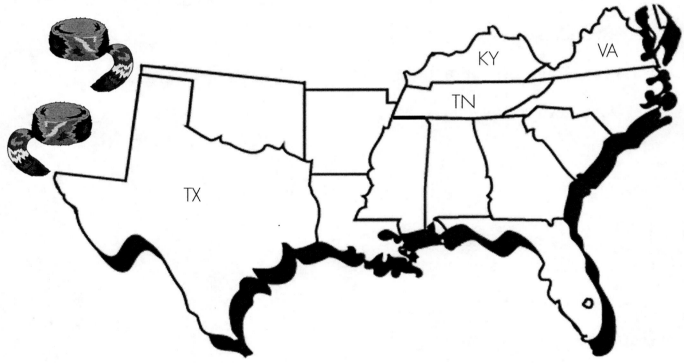

Place the following symbols in the locations indicated.

\# = where Davy Crockett was born.

* = where Davy Crockett trailed cattle.

X = where Davy Crockett served 2 terms in Congress.

! = where Davy Crockett died.

State Stuff Jumbles

See if you can unscramble the words below to get the scoop on all the state symbols of Texas.

1. FINSIREDHP _____ STATE MOTTO
2. ANCEP _____ STATE TREE
3. LGTIGIHNN KLEHW _____ STATE SHELL
4. OACMNRH TTERBUFLY _____ STATE INSECT
5. LHGNOORN _____ STATE LARGE MAMMAL
6. DILLOARMA _____ STATE SMALL MAMMAL
7. EETSW SATEX NIONO _____ STATE VEGETABLE
8. CILIH _____ STATE DISH
9. SATEX DER FRUITGRAPE _____ STATE FRUIT
10. OATSSIDE MAGRA _____ STATE GRASS
11. LUEB ZAPOT _____ STATE GEM
12. PETFIEDRIF MWOODPAL _____ STATE STONE
13. SATEX RUO SATEX _____ STATE SONG
14. ARESQU ANCED _____ STATE FOLK DANCE
15. TINUSA _____ STATE CAPITAL
16. RIBKOMGNICD _____ STATE BIRD
17. NETNOBLUBE _____ STATE FLOWER
18. EODOR _____ STATE SPORT
19. GPEADULUA SABS _____ STATE FISH
20. LAOJPEÑA _____ STATE PEPPER

ANSWERS: 1. friendship, 2. pecan, 3. lightning whelk, 4. Monarch butterfly, 5. longhorn, 6. armadillo, 7. sweet Texas onion, 8. chili, 9. red grapefruit, 10. sideoat grama, 11. blue topaz, 12. petrified palmwood, 13. Texas our Texas, 14. square dance, 15. Austin, 16. mockingbird, 17. bluebonnet, 18. rodeo, 19. guadalupe bass, 20. jalapeño

SIX FLAGS OVER TEXAS

Listed below are the different governments which have controlled Texas. The dates they controlled Texas are shown next to the name of the country.

1519-1685	**Spain**
1861-1865	**Confederate States of America**
1865-present	**United States (again and still)**
1685-1690	**France**
1690-1821	**Spain (again)**
1821-1836	**Mexico**
1836-1845	**Republic of Texas**
1845-1861	**United States**

Write the names of the countries that controlled Texas in the correct order.

1. _____

2. _____

3. _____

4. _____

5. _____

6. _____

7. _____

8. _____

Answers: 1. Spain; 2. France; 3. Spain; 4. Mexico; 5. Republic of Texas; 6. United States; 7. Confederate States of America; 8. United States

Unique Texas Place Names

Can you match the double-word names of these Texas cities and towns?
Use a map or an atlas to help you figure out the answers.

1. Aransas	A. City
2. Fort	B. Springs
3. San	C. Park
4. Lake	D. Blanca
5. League	E. Pass
6. Farmers	F. Worth
7. Corpus	G. Marcos
8. Sulphur	H. Branch
9. Deer	I. Jackson
10. Sierra	J. Christi

Answers: 1.E, 2.F, 3.G, 4.I, 5.A, 6.H, 7.J, 8.B, 9.C, 10.D.

Texas State Song

The beautiful lyrics of "Texas, Our Texas" are enriched with meaning.
Read the lyrics for the state song, and answer the questions below.

"Texas, Our Texas"
Words by Gladys Yoakum Wright and William J. Marsh,
Music by William J. Marsh

Texas, our Texas! All hail the mighty State!
Texas, our Texas! So wonderful, so great!
Boldest and grandest, withstanding every test
O empire wide and glorious,
  you stand supremely blest.

God bless you, Texas! And keep you brave and strong,
That you may grow in power and worth,
  throughout the ages long.

Texas, O Texas! Your freeborn single star,
Sends out its radiance to nations near and far.
Emblem of freedom! It sets our hearts aglow,
With thoughts of San Jacinto and glorious Alamo.
Texas, dear Texas! From tyrant grip now free,
Shines forth in splendor your star of destiny!
Mother of Heroes! We come your children true,
Proclaiming our allegiance, our faith,
  our love for you.

Explain how the "freeborn single star" could refer to the state nickname.

_____

_____

_____

Why was the battle of San Jacinto important to Texans?

_____

_____

_____

Pirate's Treasure!

Pirate Jean Lafitte came to Galveston Island in 1817. He and his brother set up a pirate camp on Snake Island called Campeachy. The Lafitte brothers raided ships, stole goods, and resold them illegally in New Orleans. In 1821, the U.S. Navy drove Lafitte out of Texas and into the Caribbean. No one knows for sure what happened to him or his ship. Do you think he had any treasure on board? Could be!

Help this treasure hunter find the gold coins.

LET'S GET REGIONAL

Texas is composed of four major land regions—the Gulf Coast Plains cover a third of the state and begin at the Gulf of Mexico. The North Central Plains gradually rise from the Gulf Coast Plain. The Great Plains are found in the Texas Panhandle. The Trans-Pecos Region is the area west of the Pecos River in the southwest corner of the state.

Color the map as follows:

Gulf Coast Plains - blue
North Central Plains - yellow
Great Plains - red
Trans-Pecos Region - green

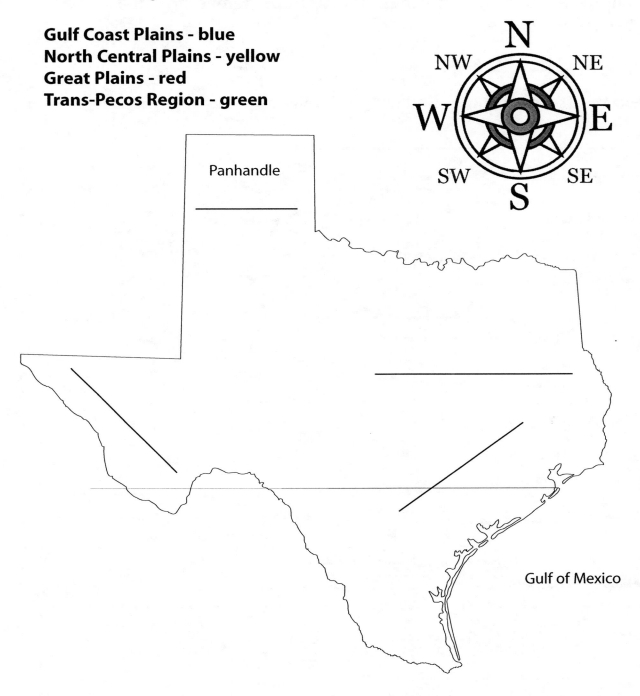

Texas
Festivals of Fun!

Texas puts on more special events than any other state. The grandest is the Texas State Fair held in Dallas during October. Many other fairs and festivals are held throughout the state, totalling about 500!

Match the fairs and festivals below with the reason for their celebration.

1. Charro Days
2. Cinco de Mayo
3. San Jacinto Days
4. Texas Citrus Festival
5. Fiesta Texas
6. Texas Cowboy Reunion and Rodeo
7. Chisholm Trail Roundups
8. Juneteenth

a. celebrate Mexican heritage
b. celebrate Texas' independence
c. honor the Mexican cowboy
d. remember cattle drive era
e. celebrate the days of the cattle trails
f. celebrate fruit harvest
g. celebrate emancipation
h. celebrate Texan cultures and music

ANSWERS: 1.c, 2.a, 3.b, 4.f, 5.h, 6.d, 7.e, 8.g

Texas Rangers

The Texas Rangers, a group of armed lawmen, were formed in1835 to provide protection against Native Americans, discourage raids by the Mexican army, and pursue cattle rustlers. On the frontier, it was said that "Texas Rangers could ride like Mexicans, shoot like Tennesseans, and fight like the very devil." Today they are no longer responsible for protecting the Texas frontier, but some Rangers still patrol remote areas on horseback and serve as special police officers for the state.

WORD BANK

FRONTIER CATTLE LAW RANGERS RUSTLERS
RAIDS PATROL ARMY HORSEBACK

```
F  R  O  N  T  I  E  R  C
I  A  K  V  C  T  M  A  A
L  I  P  A  R  M  Y  N  T
A  D  S  K  C  V  I  G  T
W  S  T  F  B  R  G  E  L
D  P  A  T  R  O  L  R  E
R  U  S  T  L  E  R  S  O
H  O  R  S  E  B  A  C  K
```

Endangered and Threatened Texas

An animal that is endangered or threatened means the animal's population numbers have declined to such a point that they could cease to exist. When animals reach this point they are placed on an endangered or threatened species list by the federal government. The endangered species laws were designed to protect the threatened animals and their homes. Texas has many animals on the endangered or threatened species list including the ocelot, red wolf, greater long-nosed bat, jaguarundi, Texas blind salamander, and Houston toad.

Use a resource, such as an encyclopedia, animal book, or the Internet, to find information on one of these six endangered animals. Make a poster to increase awareness about this animal's threatened status. Be creative!

Example:

©2006 Carole Marsh/Gallopade International/800-536-2GET/www.texasexperience.com/Page 73

A Texas Basketful

Match the name of each crop or product from Texas with the picture of the item.

Sweet Potatoes   Dairy Products   Tomatoes   Eggs

Crabs and Fish   Corn, Potatoes, Onions, and Peppers

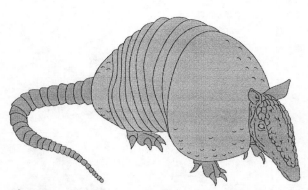

The Amiable Armadillo

The Texas state small mammal is the armadillo. They have a defensive suit of armor already built in! Some armadillos can roll themselves into a ball, so that they are completely covered in their armor. Their tongues are sticky like anteaters' tongues. That's how they pick up their food. Armadillos are usually nocturnal, which means they only come out at night. The legs and claws of the armadillo are especially suited for digging. Armadillos can bury themselves faster than you can chase them!

Fill in the blanks below using the word bank.

WORD BANK

night

suit of armor

legs

nocturnal

tongue

1. _ _ _ _ _O

2._ _ _O _ _ _ _ _ _ _

3. _ _ _O_

4. _ _ _O_ _ _ _

5. _O_ _

Now unscramble the "bubble" letters to discover the mystery word in the sentence below:

Armadillos have few or no __ __ __ __ __ !

Operation Conservation!

Soil and water conservation is an important issue facing Texans today. About twenty percent of Texas soil is considered "prime farmland," and is important to Texas' economy. Much of the rest of the state is used as rangeland for cattle and sheep grazing. Water is also an important resource. The western part of Texas receives less rain than the eastern part. West Texas is likely to be very dry, unless you're in the fertile Rio Grande valley. People in Texas have built dams to create reservoirs of water, and wells to reach water well below the surface. Developers look for ways to create buildings, homes, bridges, and dams. Sometimes they disturb natural habitats. Preservationists try to preserve natural habitats in their present state. They prefer to leave nature alone. Do you think there is a way for them to work together?

Look at the two columns below. Try to write two reasons under each column to support each cause.

Developers	**Preservationists**
_____	_____
_____	_____

Now that you have looked at both viewpoints, what group would you support in the future?

Why do you feel this way? _____

_____

_____

_____

Howdy Buckaroo!

"My name is Buck. I help herd the longhorns that roam the Texas Plains. I live on different ranches and often make camp on the trail. Our horses have funny names like Paint Spot and Willy. I've heard longhorns first arrived when Spanish ships brought them from Europe. Gracias!"

Color the Longhorn brown.
Color Buck's vest, chaps and bandanna.
Add spots to Buck's favorite pony, Paint Spot!

Spanish Exploration

Álvar Núñez Cabeza de Vaca wandered through Texas from 1528-1536. He and his fellow shipmates were held as slaves by Native Americans before finding Spanish settlements. The Spanish were the first Europeans to explore the state of Texas. They were lured here by stories of cities of gold and jewels. In 1540, Francisco Vásquez de Coronado led an expedition to discover the Seven Cities of Cibola and Quivira. The group wandered through West Texas and East New Mexico, but they never found the mythical "cities of gold."

Color the Spanish Explorers below.

Cinco de Mayo

The fifth day of May is known as Cinco de Mayo. It is a special day of celebration for Mexican Americans in Texas. It is a special day set aside to celebrate their heritage with parades and parties. Many people think it is the anniversary of Mexico's independence, but it isn't. That day is September 16, known as Diez y Seis, which commemorates the beginning of Mexico's War of Independence from Spain in 1810. Mexico finally won their independence in 1821.

Color the picture.

Rodeo Roundup

Rodeos were a form a competition and entertainment for cowboys in the late 1800s. Since cowboy life was very rough and tough, rodeos provided a fun way to be entertained and to show off their skills as cowboys. Still today, rodeos are very much a part of true Texas. Some rodeo events include barrel racing, stunt riding, bronco riding, bullriding, roping and bulldogging. Both men and women participate in the events.

Complete the bubblegram below, using the words in the Word Bank to help you.

WORD BANK
RODEO
COWBOY
LASSO
BRONCO
STUNT

1. R ◯ __ __ __
2. ◯ __ S S __
3. ◯ T __ __ __ __
4. ◯ __ ◯ __ __ __ Y
5. B __ __ ◯ __ __

Now unscramble the bubble letters to discover the Mystery Word!

Mystery Word: ____ ____ ____ ____ ____ ____
(The silly rodeo participants)

Texas Twisters!

The lovely landscape of Texas' gulf coast has gentle breezes and beautiful beaches. It's hard to believe that terrible natural disasters can strike this beautiful paradise.

See if you can uncover some of the natural disasters that affect the state of Texas. Use the Word Bank below to help you unscramble the following words:

1. oodlf   _ _ _ _ _ _

2. lhia   _ _ _ _ _

3. rrhunieac   _ _ _ _ _ _ _ _ _

4. hbrsu reif   _ _ _ _ _ _ _ _ _ _

5. der dtei   _ _ _ _ _ _ _ _

6. qmsuotio   _ _ _ _ _ _ _ _

7. tsrfo   _ _ _ _ _

8. notorad   _ _ _ _ _ _ _

9. qethkaruea   _ _ _ _ _ _ _ _ _ _

10. twspareuot   _ _ _ _ _ _ _ _ _ _

WORD BANK

tornado

earthquake

brush fire

mosquito

hurricane

red tide

waterspout

hail

flood

frost

States All Around!
Code-Buster

Decipher the code and write in the names of the states near Texas.

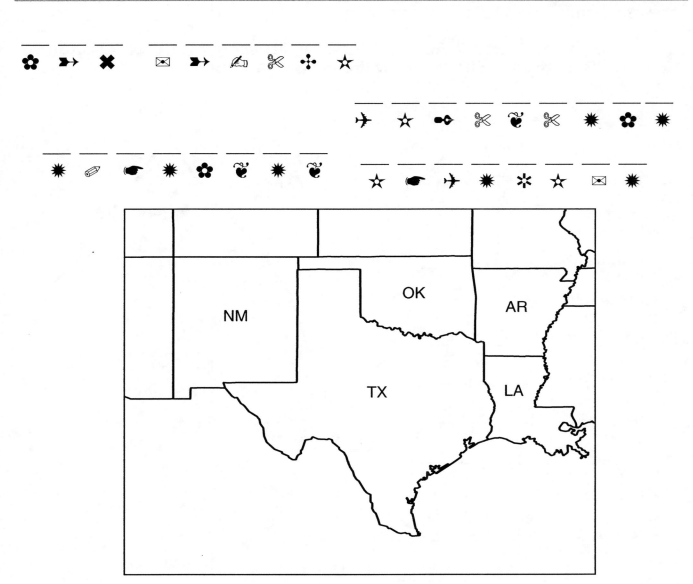

Texas Cities

Circle Austin in red. It is our state's capital. The star is the map symbol for our capital.

Circle San Antonio in yellow. The Alamo is in San Antonio. **Draw a** 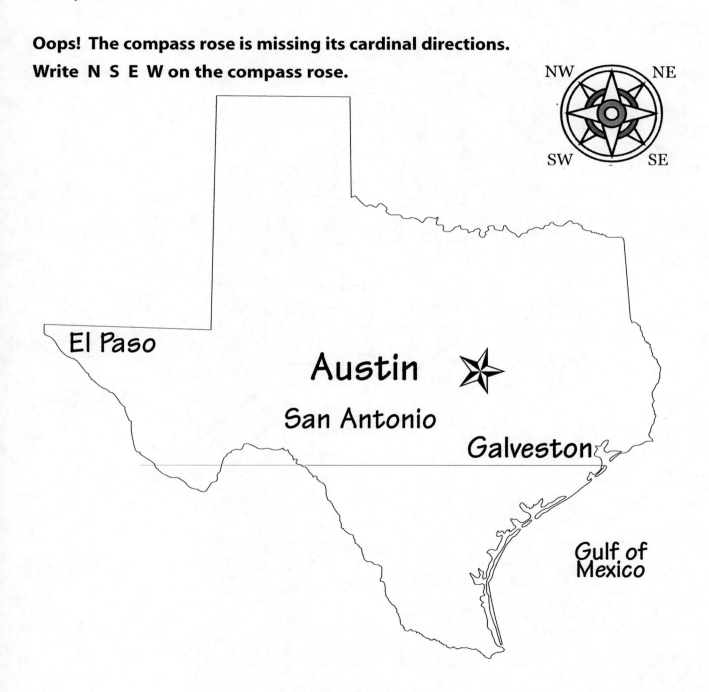 **symbol near San Antonio**

Circle Galveston in blue. It is close to the Gulf of Mexico.

Circle El Paso in brown. It is close to New Mexico.

Add your city or town to the map if it's not here. Circle it in green. Give it a ⊙ **symbol to show you live there.**

Oops! The compass rose is missing its cardinal directions.

Write N S E W on the compass rose.

NW   NE

SW   SE

El Paso

Austin ★

San Antonio

Galveston

Gulf of
Mexico

Texas,
A Quilt of Many Counties

Texas has 254 counties. To make a "quilt" of your state, use different colored markers or crayons to shade in the counties. Write in the name of your county, town, and your state's capital. Color your county red. Color the counties around yours blue.

WOW!
What a colorful quilt!

Similar Symbols

Texas has many symbols including a state small mammal, bird, tree, dish, shell, and flag. **Circle the items in each row that is not a symbol of Texas.**

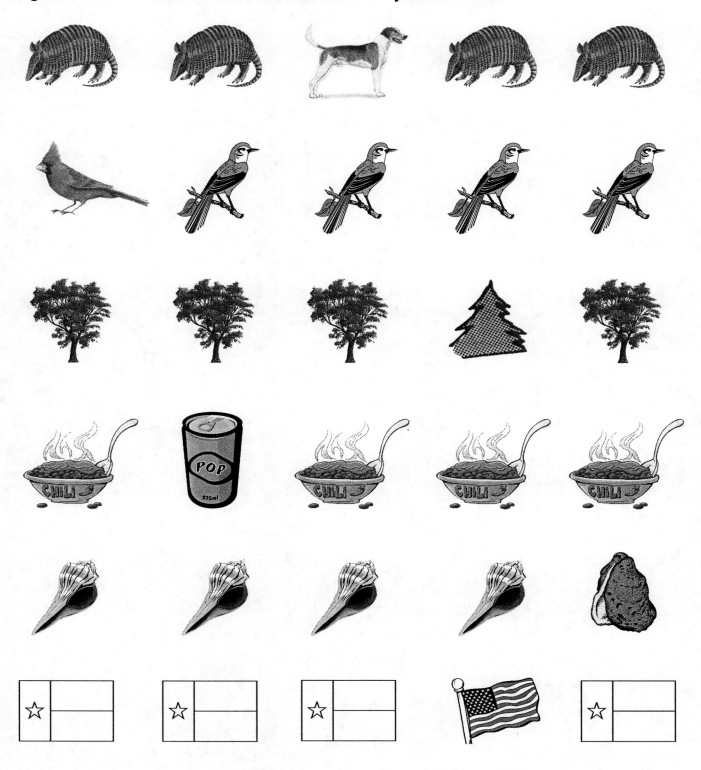

Texas Grows the Most!

Over 100 species of cacti are Texas residents–ouch! Sometimes they have pretty flowers growing on them. Color these cacti, and decorate them with colorful blooms.

What Shall I Wear?

In early Texas, settlers dressed much as you do now. Styles were influenced by the Spanish settlers. Even cowboys' clothes were influenced by the Spanish.

Draw a line from each word to its correct place on the characters.

Chaps

Stetson Hat

Vest

Dress

Sash

Blouse

Bandanna

Ribbons

Boots

Whiskers

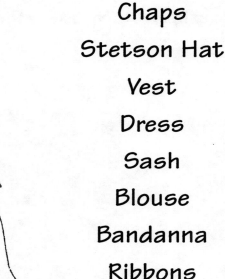

In frontier times, cats did not wear clothes!

U.S. Time Zones

Would you believe that the continental United States is divided into four time zones? It is! Because of the rotation of the earth, the sun travels from east to west. Whenever the sun is directly overhead a city, we call that time noon. But, when it is noon in Peoria, the sun has a long way to go before it is directly over, say, Sacramento, California. In other words, it can't be noon in every place at the same time! This explains the reason the continental United States has four time zones. For example, when it is 12:00 pm (noon) in Miami, it is 11:00 am in Houston, Texas. Did you notice there is a one-hour time difference between each zone?

Look at the time zones on the map below, then answer the following questions:

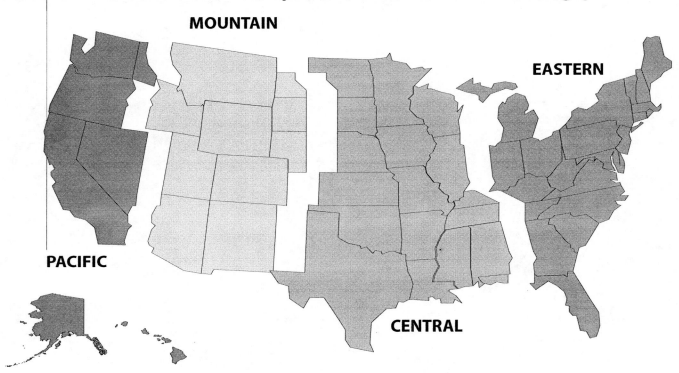

1. When it is 10:00 am in Texas what time is it in Georgia? _____ am

2. When it is 3:30 pm in Austin, Texas what time is it in Kansas? _____ pm

3. What time zone is Texas located in? _____

4. What time zone is California in? _____

5. If it is 10:00 pm in Dallas, Texas, what time is it in California? _____ pm

Answers: 1. 9:00 am, 2. 3:30 pm, 3. Central, 4. Pacific, 5. 8:00 pm

Early Native Americans Abound!

The first people ever to reach the land that would one day become the state of Texas may have traveled across a frozen bridge of land linking Asia to North America. This continent to continent walk may have taken place as long as 30,000 years ago! After they reached Texas, Native Americans continued to travel and improve their way of life.

Complete the matching activity below.

1. Caddo Tribe

2. wandering hunters

3. because they had no horses, they traveled…

4. village homes

5. crops grown

6. seashells, copper, and minerals

7. Hasinai

8. Cherokee

A. fought settlers in 1839 at Neches River

B. corn and squash

C. nomads

D. used in trading as money

E. early Texas Native American group

F. on foot

G. Native Americans who named Texas

H. domed houses of wood, grass, mud, or animal skins

Would you like to work on an archaeological dig?

Answers: 1.G, 2.C, 3.F, 4.H, 5.B, 6.D, 7.E, 8.A

Texas State Flower, The Bluebonnet

Every state has a favorite flower. The Texas state flower is the Bluebonnet. The Bluebonnet is a plant with compound leaves and clusters of blue flowers.

Color the picture of our state flower.

I ♥ Texas!

The last battle of the Civil War was fought at Palmito Ranch, near Brownsville.

Texas is the nation's leader in the production of cotton, cattle, sheep, wool, natural gas, oil, salt, and sulphur.

Texas was its own country for 10 years before it became a state.

Texas is one of many states whose name was taken from an Indian word. *Tejas* is a Caddo word that means "Friend."

Texas has had 6 national flags flying over it: those of Spain, France, Mexico, the Republic of Texas, the Confederacy, and the U.S.

Texas can legally split itself into five states, if it wants to, under the terms of its annexation agreement.

Texas has the most drive-in theaters of any state.

In Texas, it was once illegal for a man to carry a pair of pliers.

Oil was first struck near Corsicana in 1894.

Many people like to visit Texas. They think it is a beautiful state and love the historic places, the beautiful scenery, and our friendly people.

Add some other facts you know about Texas here:

_____

_____

T Is For Texas

T is for Ten-gallon cowboy hats

E is for El Capitan

X is for XIT Ranch

A is for the Alamo

S is for the Sunsets

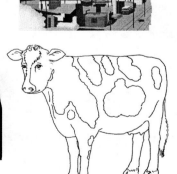

Now see if you can make up your own acrostic poem describing your city or town. Be sure to use words that best describe what sets your town apart from all the others in Texas.

Old Man River

Texas has many great rivers. Rivers give us water for our crops. Rivers are also water "highways." On these water highways travel crops, manufactured goods, people, and many other things—including children in tire tubes!

Here are some of Texas' most important rivers:

SABINE	RIO GRANDE	RED
CANADIAN	PECOS	TRINITY
SAN ANTONIO	BRAZOS	GUADALUPE

Draw someone "tubing" down a Texas River!

Ollie's Orange Grove

Ollie grows oranges in Texas' fertile and warm Rio Grande Valley. Orange trees need a warm, moist climate to survive and produce delicious oranges. Texas ranks third in the country in the production of oranges and grapefruit. The only states who produce more are Florida and California.

How many oranges do you see in Ollies' grove? ☐

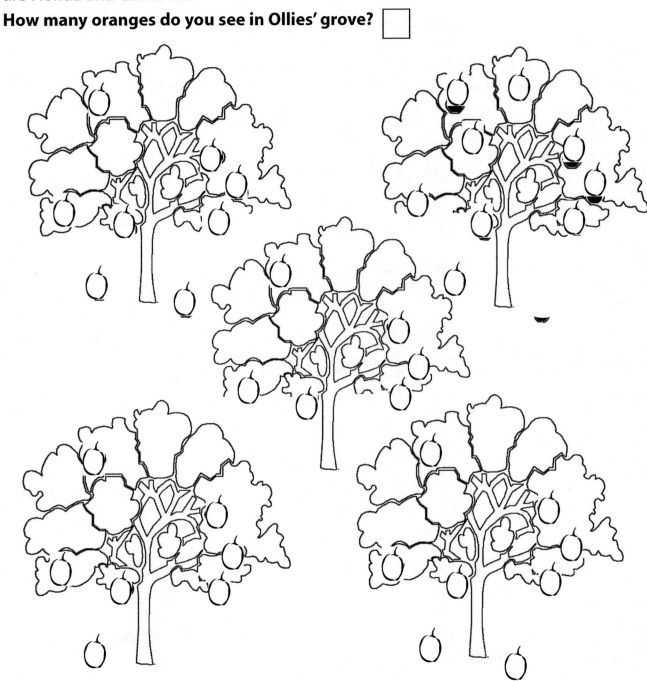

The Rio Grande Valley in southern Texas has an eleven month growing season.

ANSWER: 38 Oranges

Know your Texas Geography!

Pop quiz! It's time to test your knowledge of Texas! Try to answer all of the questions before you look at the answers.

1. Stephen Austin originally brought _____ families to settle in Texas.
    - ○ a) 30
    - ○ b) 300
    - ○ c) 3,000

2. Texas was an independent nation for:
    - ○ a) 6 months
    - ○ b) 100 years
    - ○ c) 10 years

3. The colony of Zodiac was settled by:
    - ○ a) Mormons
    - ○ b) astrologers
    - ○ c) German settlers

4. The first day this famous lawman was in El Paso, he saw two men killed within one-half hour:
    - ○ a) John Selman
    - ○ b) Jesse James
    - ○ c) Wyatt Earp

5. More than 250 species of what are found in Texas waters?
    - ○ a) shrimp
    - ○ b) fish
    - ○ c) oysters

6. What tree grows to only 12-18 inches (30-45 centimeters) tall?
    - ○ a) Shin Oak
    - ○ b) Quaking Aspen
    - ○ c) Juniper

7. Monohans is the center for capturing:
    - ○ a) bees
    - ○ b) birds
    - ○ c) fleas

8. Half of the world's supply of what is produced by Texas' goats?
    - ○ a) goat's milk
    - ○ b) goat leather
    - ○ c) mohair

9. The Kimbell Museum houses an art collection in this city:
    - ○ a) Dallas
    - ○ b) Forth Worth
    - ○ c) Beaumont

10. Chief Yellow Bear died of:
    - ○ a) malnutrition
    - ○ b) gas asphyxiation
    - ○ c) an arrow wound

Answers: 1-b; 2-c; 3-a; 4-c; 5-b; 6-a; 7-c; 8-c; 9-b; 10-b

Texas Two-Step

How many of these two-name places can you match? You might need a map or an atlas to help you figure them out.

Two For The Price Of One!

1. Big

2. Buffalo

3. Chisholm

4. Clear

5. Pecos

6. Comanche

7. Corpus

8. Diablo

9. Fort

10. Galveston

11. Johnson

12. New

13. Palo

14. Port

15. San

A. Bliss

B. River

C. Alto

D. Bayou

E. Antonio

F. Springs

G. Island

H. Trail

I. Braunfels

J. Christi

K. Bend

L. Arthur

M. Mountains

N. Lake

O. City

Answers: 1-K; 2-D; 3-H; 4-N; 5-B; 6-F; 7-J; 8-M; 9-A; 10-G; 11-O; 12-I; 13-C; 14-L; 15-E